Confronting Your Clutter

By Carolyn Koehnline, M.A., L.M.H.C.

Dedicated to all the students, clients, friends, family and colleagues who have generously contributed to my understanding of this multi-faceted topic.

Published by:
Carolyn Koehnline
PO Box 6091
Bellingham, WA 98227-6091

Library of Congress Control Number: 2010905962

ISBN: 976-0-692-00927-7

The purpose of this book is to educate, inform and enlighten those persons who wish to use the exercises and essays for self-knowledge and personal growth. It is not meant to replace psychological or medical treatment.

Carolyn can be contacted through her website: www.ConfrontingClutter.com

Introduction

Clutter is the excess stuff we tend to accumulate in our homes, our heads, our hearts, and our schedules.

I first got intrigued by clutter when I was in graduate school. While studying to be a therapist and learning to look at the world through psychological eyes, I was making my living cleaning houses. I spent many hours a day meditatively scrubbing and dusting other peoples' homes and belongings.

As I worked I noticed how people lived, how they inhabited their spaces, and how they dealt with their possessions. I began noticing their clutter. This was interesting to me because I struggled with it too. Behind closed doors I also had piles of papers, a closet with too many clothes that didn't fit me anymore and objects that had no real home. I was relieved to find that many intelligent, interesting, delightful people seemed to be struggling in a similar way.

The more I got interested in clutter, the more I began talking about it with my housecleaning clients and my friends. While vacuuming and polishing I also had long stretches of introspective time to examine my own clutter patterns.

I became aware that while some people seemed burdened by the sheer presence of too many things—too much furniture, too many dishes, too many plastic containers without lids, even more seemed burdened by *mental clutter*. They were overwhelmed. Their brains were overloaded with the number of decisions they had to make in a day, the different roles they were playing and the burden of responsibilities that came with all of those roles. They were too overwhelmed to deal with the paperwork piling up around them. Their appointment books were bursting with too many appointments and obligations. I carefully stacked the magazines, books and professional journals heaped by their bedside tables. I folded the rumpled clothes forgotten on the tops of their dryers. I sponged around the insistent sticky notes clinging to their refrigerator doors.

During such times I thought about how the culture I live in teaches us that we are supposed to be constantly consuming. We should be endlessly absorbing information. More gadgets will make our lives easier. More things will make us happier. The faster we move the further ahead we'll get. We are not taught to value open spaces, or quiet, or rest, or the unscheduled time it takes to reflect, digest and make meaning of our experiences.

As I continued my housecleaning career, my study of clutter became ever more refined. I noticed that in addition to *mental clutter,* I and many of my housecleaning clients were also weighed down by *emotional clutter.* We were holding onto things that represented unresolved chapters of our lives. We were stuffing artifacts from past professions or relationships or identities into boxes, and shoving them into corners.

I thought about how my culture is very good at teaching us how to accumulate things, but not very good at teaching us anything about how to let go of possessions or loved ones or homes or jobs. To let go means to consciously say, "Good bye," and to open up space. For many of us, that is a terrifying proposition. We don't tend to experience open space as delicious *spaciousness*, full of mystery and possibility. For many of us it is a frightening *emptiness* to be avoided at all costs.

These observations and thoughts planted a seed that eventually grew into the "Confronting Clutter" class. After I completed my master's degree in psychology and made the shift from housecleaner to therapist, I felt drawn to design a class to help people release their clutter. I combined my psychological training with my direct observations and experiences, and read everything I could find on the subject. Eight people attended that first class and I will always be grateful to them.

The class became an opportunity to explore in depth the mental and emotional nuances of clutter and the underlying conflicts it represents. I addressed issues such as procrastination, making choices, moving through transitions, navigating time, letting go, and simplifying life. I wanted to counteract the notion that our problems can all be solved if we just accumulate more stuff, engage in more activities, or gather more information. At that time, and ever since, one of the central ideas in my teaching has been that *it is often spaciousness that is most needed — more space in our homes, heads, hearts and schedules.*

This collection of essays and exercises is a distillation of what I have learned from many years of teaching that class and numerous workshops on clutter-related topics. Each group of people that has gathered to learn and share has added to my understanding of what is helpful to the process of Confronting Clutter.

This is not a detailed how-to book about getting organized. *Confronting Your Clutter* is for those who may not feel ready or willing to follow someone else's system in any kind of consistent way, but who no longer want to ignore the issue. My intention is to inspire, encourage, and to evoke "ahas!"

Over the years I have noticed that often when people begin to understand what's been going on in their relationship with their clutter, they also begin to release accumulated shame. This opens up creativity and inspiration. They open to finding ways of solving their own clutter conflicts. They also become more able to access the kinds of support that are truly helpful to them.

You may find this collection will be all you need to get yourself focused and moving, addressing your clutter situation in your own way. If you need further assistance, you may want to link up with a friend, take a class, or hire a professional organizer or clutter consultant. You'll probably want to give yourself the kinds of support that have helped you make positive changes in the past. I encourage you to refer to the resource list.

If your clutter is a byproduct of a bigger issue, you will need to address that in order to make progress. Disabilities, illnesses, and mood disorders can all affect one's attention span, energy level, and organizational abilities. They can increase the likelihood of accumulating clutter and make it more challenging to confront it.

If you are an adult with attention deficit disorder you will need to find the proper balance of medications, remedies and strategies to help your brain function at its best. You may need to work with a doctor, psychiatrist, holistic practitioner, and/or counselor. If you are suffering from depression, anxiety, trauma, or bereavement, you may require psychotherapy, a support group, medication, or body work to help you to get a foothold. You'll need to figure out what supports will allow you to have the energy, focus and persistence required for the Confronting Clutter process.

Whatever your combination of strengths and challenges, if you have the right kinds of help, Confronting Your Clutter is possible. It does not have to be an exercise in self-torture. My hope is that it will give you practice loving and respecting yourself even when you're face-to-face with your imperfections.

Confronting Your Clutter can also be an opportunity to practice courage. By taking the risk of releasing your grip on belongings, thoughts, and attachments that are no longer helpful to you, your hands can be open to receive the unexpected gifts that are coming your way.

A Closer
Look at
Clutter

Confronting Clutter

"Just get rid of it."
That's what the books all say.
They cheerfully pronounce it with such
pluck and confidence
it makes me think it
should
be easy.
After all, it's just
stuff.

I
should
be able to take a weekend,
focus in,
and deal with it once and for all.

But even to look is scary
when I've gotten so good at blinding myself to
postponed decisions, unfinished tasks,
objects skulking around without a real home.

My clutter is a container for
thoughts I don't want to think and
feelings I don't want to feel.

To show up, open my eyes,
and do what needs to be done
requires that I call upon my most
valiant, courageous, heroic self.

If you call this simple, you are setting me up for failure.
If you call this simple, you are belittling the dangers of this
adventure.

I am willing to show up, look with open eyes,
and do what needs to be done,
but I am not willing
to pretend that it's
simple.

What is Clutter?

Clutter is subjective. One person's clutter is another person's treasure. What is valuable to me in one chapter of my life may be clutter in another chapter. Therefore, it can be confusing to try and figure out what is clutter and what is not.

I say it's clutter if it . . .

>   drains my energy

>   gets in my way

>   distracts me from what is important to me or

>   doesn't have a real place or use in my home or my life.

Just because it looks chaotic doesn't necessarily mean that it is clutter. When I am using my art supplies I'm sure it would look like a disaster to the outsider. I know that those materials are giving me energy, feeding my dreams and are an active part of my life. Those supplies all have homes, and I'll be putting them back into those homes when I'm finished. What about all those neatly stacked fabric squares arranged by color? They may be clutter if I'm never going to use them, and if they are bringing up feelings of guilt every time I walk by them.

Physical clutter includes plastic containers without lids, clothes that don't fit, tools that don't work, leftovers from projects I meant to do but never started, and from those I started but never completed. It includes the dead refrigerator out in the garage. It's the macramé butterfly that never really fit my taste, but it was a gift so I thought I had to keep it. It's the boxes from all the appliances and electronic equipment I've ever purchased. It's the socks without mates and the half-knitted sweater that started getting mysteriously wider with each row.

It is also the piles and piles of paper! All that paper pours into my life and looks almost exactly alike. Some of it is extremely important and to ignore it has dire consequences. Some of it is totally worthless. Most of it falls into that vague, in-between category of "Well, I might need this someday. I'm not sure." I pile it up. I spread it out. I stuff it into grocery bags, hoping that someday I'll know what to do with it.

Mental clutter is the excess baggage I carry around in my head. It includes worries, shaming, blaming, over-analyzing. It takes up space in my brain that could be better used for other things. Mental clutter accumulates when I don't take the time and energy to stop and listen to myself to get clear about what is important to me. It piles up when I postpone crucial decisions. It's there when I'm feeling overwhelmed.

Old belief systems that have outlived their usefulness are also mental clutter. When I tell myself I'm not smart enough or that I'm bound to fail, I am not really thinking. I'm just replaying old messages that have made well-worn grooves in my brain.

I need to take a break and collect myself, get some fresh air or a drink of water. I may need to pose a question to myself in my journal, and see what answers come. Instead I flood myself with chatter that gets me nowhere.

Emotional clutter is the excess baggage I carry around in my heart. My culture encourages me to move quickly from one thing to the next. When I endure changes, losses, traumas, disappointments, injustices, I'm expected to keep going, and to keep showing up for the next thing. I may have a heart filled with sorrow, anger, fear, guilt, and other feelings considered unacceptable by polite company.

It would be healthiest for me to acknowledge the feelings, express them in safe ways, use them as fuel to make positive changes, move them out of my body. Instead, I may just try to ignore them. That doesn't work. They don't go away. They show up later as a lack of energy, a sense of disconnection, or perpetual anger that comes out at the slightest thing. They can turn into depression, anxiety, physical problems, or a cutting off from my natural joy and creativity. If I have a back-log of these upsetting emotions I may shut down my feelings altogether, keeping busy so that I don't have any quiet time when they could possibly emerge.

Time clutter is the excess baggage in my schedule. When I am unintentional with my day and it fills up with things that are not ultimately helpful or satisfying, that is time clutter. It is there when I lose hours to emailing, text messaging, phoning, TV-watching, or shopping. It appears when I don't plan well, and perpetually overfill my schedule.
In addition to my own confusions with time, I may work at a job or live in a family where planning, reflection, and closure are not encouraged or supported. It may be normal for me to be constantly interrupted. This can

cause me to lose track of what's important to me, and leave me vulnerable to other people's dramas and my own mindless escapes. When I am bombarded with too many things and lose track of my own priorities, decisions about time can become a confusing blur. Time is precious, but I can forget to treat it that way.

Physical, mental, emotional and time clutter are not neatly separated categories. A cluttered space depresses me and scatters my thinking. A cluttered mind keeps me from making clear choices on my own behalf. When my heart is cluttered, I have difficulty knowing what to keep and what to let go. A cluttered schedule means I'm always running out the door late, feeling fragmented, distracted, and leaving a disaster in my wake. All of these categories are closely interrelated.

To make progress with my clutter I need to begin to understand how this whole mixed bag operates in my life. This can happen a little at a time, as I'm ready for each step. Fortunately, letting go of any clutter in any category opens the way to releasing more of it.

My Clutter

Clutter is my protection.
Stay away. Keep out. This is my space.

Clutter is my friend.
Familiar. Soothing. Amusing. Safe.

Clutter is my memory.
I've done things, seen things. People have known me.

Clutter is my anger.
I scatter pieces of myself throughout the house because I'm furious I have no real space of my own.

Clutter is my creativity.
I see the beauty and potential in everything!

Clutter is a shameful reminder.
It shows me all the ways I don't measure up to who I think I should be.

Clutter is my ungrieved losses.
It is the resentments, wounds, devastations I carry with me in boxes because I'm not ready to let them go.

Clutter is my fear of making a decision.
I can't choose, so I try to choose everything.

Clutter is my loose ends.
I hang onto the props hoping that someday I'll actually finish something.

Clutter is false soul food.
It pretends to fill, but always leaves me hungry.

Clutter is my mixed feelings.
I want it and I don't want it.
There's no place to put it,
but how can I let it end up in a landfill?

Specific Things to Try

Complete the following sentences, avoiding the tendency to belabor your answers. Trust whatever comes in the moment.

My physical clutter includes_____

_____

The mental clutter I'm aware of in myself includes_____

_____

The emotional clutter I'm aware of in myself includes_____

_____

My time gets cluttered with _____

_____

The kind of clutter that is the biggest issue for me at this time in my life is

_____

_____

If I had less of this kind of clutter in my life I would_____

_____

Use the phrase, *"Underneath my clutter . . ."* as a springboard to writing. Keep writing the phrase and finishing the sentence, writing quickly so that you don't stop and edit your thoughts. For example: *Underneath my clutter is a lot of confusion about what I want. Underneath my clutter is open space. Underneath my clutter I'm afraid there won't be enough.*

Underneath my clutter . . .

List types of physical clutter that you tend to accumulate:

_____

_____

_____

_____

_____

_____

Now try the *Underneath my clutter* exercise, but replace the word *clutter* with a specific kind of clutter each time you write the sentence. *Underneath my paper . . . Underneath my clothes that no longer fit . . .* Once again, write quickly, don't think too much and don't censor. The unexpected thoughts are often the most enlightening.

Underneath my

Underneath my

Underneath my

Underneath my

Underneath my

Preparations

Inspiring Myself

I begin with stillness.
Stillness, and my own breath.

Bringing my focus to the space I want to transform
I see piles of obligations I've been trying to avoid.

It is tempting to give in to shame.

Seeing those piles of
guilt,
heaviness,
stuck, immovable energy,
it is tempting to run, hide, busy myself, bury myself,
to become a rebellious two-year-old
or a limp rag.

I come back to the breath,
inhale,
exhale,
and begin to imagine this space exactly as I want it to be.

I see the heaviness lifting,
the stuck energy beginning to move,
the excess baggage recycled,
redistributed,
released back into the world in helpful, harmless forms.

Breathing,
focusing,
I imagine this space in glorious detail,
organized in ways that fit how my brain thinks,
with the colors and smells that make me feel good
and with just enough of the things that
nourish me,
delight me,
and fit exactly the person I most want to be.

Myself.

The Soul House

Inside each of us there is a house. It is the one we yearn for. It is the place where we would feel truly at home.

What is it like, this house of mine? Is it more like a castle, or more like a cottage? A lighthouse? A farmhouse? A skyscraper condominium?

What is it like inside this house? Is it sparse and serene? Is it warm and abundant? Is it an active house with creative projects in the making and interesting things to pick up, each having its own story? Is it simple, intentional, and clear? Does everything have a real place to be where it can sit comfortably and be found easily when it is needed, or is everything having a wild party, getting all mixed up in unexpected ways?

How does time run in this house? Is there a comfortable routine? Do things occur predictably and in their proper order, or is it spontaneous and surprising? Do the minutes click along like clockwork, or does time stretch out in a slow, dreamy way?

What happens here? Do musical instruments get played? Do special corners get savored with a good book? Does the table often have friends around it? Or is it mainly a home base for adventures out in the world; a place to stop in and re-pack my bag while grabbing a snack and heading out the door?

Who lives here and how do they treat each other? Do I live alone? With a partner? Family? Friends? Are there children? Animals? Growing things? Does each person have their own space with privacy carefully respected, or is it more of a free-for-all with all spaces open to everybody? Is it a boisterous house filled with belly laughs and singing and passionate arguments? Or is it a calm, gentle, subtle space filled with deep listening and long stretches of quiet? Is it sensuous and romantic? Is somebody canning plums? Is there a mad scientist in the basement?

I allow myself to imagine this house. Not the one I would settle for. Not the one others tell me I should want. I am imagining my true house, my Soul House. To begin to imagine it is to begin to make it real.

Specific Things to Try

Write, draw, sing, dance or tell someone about your *Soul House* in all its glorious detail. Don't worry about making it the perfect description. Just write whatever comes today, in this moment. Be sure and get into it with all of your senses, and don't let yourself be limited by what is, "realistic." This is an exploration to begin to get a sense of what you want.

My Soul House

Next, pick out four words that sum up the essential qualities of your Soul House. For example: *beauty, simplicity, creativity, community, sensuousness, practicality, efficiency, light, freedom, order, privacy, spontaneity,* Resist the temptation to choose more than four words.

1. _____

2. _____

3. _____

4. _____

Finally, think about your current living space and ask yourself if you have enough *spaciousness* or *light* or *warmth* or *practicality* (or whatever your four words were) in that space. If not, what are some specific changes you can make in your current environment to bring more of those qualities into your life?

Choose one cluttered room. Do a drawing or diagram of how you'd like it to look and feel. You don't have to know every detail and you don't have to be a great artist. Just see what comes, right now, in this moment. You can always change it later. Feel free to add descriptive words. Be sure you are bringing in some of the qualities you listed at the bottom of page 19.

Gathering Support

Being a Helpful Boss to Myself

When I am confronting my clutter, I am self-employed. I am the one determining what I will work on, and for how long. I am the one in charge of rewarding or reprimanding. I am the one who is ultimately responsible for what happens. That means I have a choice as to whether I am going to be a helpful boss or an unhelpful boss.

Unfortunately, I have experienced some unhelpful bosses. They were the ones who managed to get me to be my most miserable and least productive self – to dread getting up in the mornings, and to watch the clock all day. They brought out my most rebellious side, or worse yet, sucked the life right out of me. How did they accomplish this? By only noticing me when I did something wrong, or picking at me, or giving me impossibly long lists of things to do and expecting me to complete them in next to no time. Or by being rigidly set on having me do things their way, when that way didn't fit me at all.

I've noticed that even now, when I'm face-to-face with my clutter, those unhelpful bosses of my past want to creep right in and take me over. When this happens, I can become my own worst enemy. The pile of papers becomes a looming mountain of impossible decisions, and I become a worthless slob who has never done anything right. I have entered The Land of the Giants. No matter what the task is before me, it seems infinitely huge, and my efforts seem puny and hopelessly inadequate. I could sort through papers forever and never make any progress.

Luckily, I have also had wonderfully helpful bosses, teachers, parents and friends who supported me in doing my best work. They were good at helping me to break things down, step by step. They paid close attention, and noticed specifically what I was doing right. They provided me with the tools I needed, and then allowed me to proceed in my own way. They believed in me, trusted me to do good work, and gave encouragement with grace and ease.

When I am crawling helplessly around in the Land of the Giants, seduced by the words of the unhelpful bosses, there is a way to break the spell and wake up from that evil enchantment. All I have to do is summon the helpful bosses of my past. I imagine them around me, and remember what it was like to feel their gentleness, their respect, and their belief in me. I give myself the encouragement they would give. I picture myself as they would see me. I break down the task into bite-sized pieces. I tell myself everything I am doing right. I give myself permission to approach the task in my own way.

Remembering the helpful bosses does not solve everything. There is still the same amount of work to do, but somehow, it doesn't feel so daunting. I no longer perceive myself to be a tiny child, or the mound of papers to be the size of Everest. Somehow, feeling the encouragement of those who have believed in me, I grow taller, and I open my eyes to a much friendlier-looking reality.

Once I have awoken and come back from the Land of the Giants, I am not thinking about helpful bosses or unhelpful bosses, punishments or rewards. The arguments in my head have ceased. I am simply getting to work, doing what needs to be done. Even though I am not particularly conscious of it, I am at peace.

Instructions for my Inner Boss

Be very specific about what the task is.
Don't trivialize or discount the work you are asking me to do.
Be realistic about the time it will require.

Give me a reasonable schedule.
Be clear about when I'm working and when I'm free.
Build in breaks.

Make my work atmosphere as comfortable as possible.
Open the curtains. Play inspiring music.
Make sure I have enough air and light.
Give me a comfortable place to sit.

Break down the job into bite-sized pieces.
Otherwise I'll get overwhelmed and feel defeated.

Allow time for me to bring closure to each portion of the task.
Don't give me new tasks until I am ready.
Encourage me to bring my current project to completion.

Express your appreciation frequently for all my hard work, out loud if possible.
Rewarding me with treats would be helpful too.

Concentrate on noticing what I have accomplished, and on inspiring me for the next step.
This will help me to keep up my momentum.

Assume that if you provide me with the proper tools, inspiration and support, I will do a good job.
Don't demand perfection. Only ask me to do my best.

A Sample Confronting Clutter Session

1. I choose one cluttered area to focus on. It could be a surface, a drawer, a cupboard, a corner. I schedule a time to work on it including a beginning and an ending time.

2. When the time comes I take a look at it. If shame comes up I say some words of self-forgiveness. Then I do my best to imagine how I'd like the area to look when I'm finished. I ask myself what kinds of things I know for sure I want to keep.

3. I assemble my supplies and place them where I can reach them easily.

   Sorting bins or boxes with bold labels:

   <u>Stays</u>: Put back into the area I'm sorting.

   <u>Relocate</u>: Deliver to another room.

   <u>File</u>: I have a stack of file folders in this one.

   <u>Needs a Home</u>: I want to keep this but don't yet know where.

   <u>Give Away/Sell</u>: I don't have to know where or how I'm getting rid of it.

   <u>Emotional</u>: Too difficult to decide about yet.

   <u>Recycle</u>
   <u>Trash</u>
   <u>Shred</u>

   Sticky Notes:
   These make quick temporary labels.

   Zip-Lock Bags:
   This is for little items, coins, pencils.

Bold Marker

Reminder Sheet:
> When I come across papers and objects that remind me of things I need to do, I don't get up and do them immediately. Instead, I write them down.

Timer:
> I can immerse in the task while it keeps track of the time.

Appointment Book or Calendar:
> A place to write down dates so I don't have to hang onto individual pieces of paper.

4. I set the timer for one third of the time I've allotted for this Confronting Clutter session. When the timer rings, I shift gears, and begin bringing closure to what I've sorted.

Relocate: I deliver the things that belong in other rooms.

File: I actually file these items. If my files are too full, I create temporary file storage in a box with the file folders stored vertically as if they were arranged in a file drawer. I can use a file cart for temporary storage until I've cleaned out my file cabinet, or use it as a permanent alternative.

Needs a Home: I do my best to create a real place for these items, or at least put them close to where I think their home will eventually be once I've had the time to create it.

Give Away/Sell: I separate these two categories. Then on my reminder sheet I figure out what I'll be doing with different items and what my next step is. I schedule a time on my calendar for following through with delivering the things I am going to donate or sell. I may also schedule a time to go on-line to connect with potential recipients or buyers using the websites on the resource list at the back of this book.

Emotional: I take another look at these items. It may be clearer what to keep and what to let go. Some things may still feel overwhelming and may require intentional emotional processing at another time. I box them up, label the box "Emotional" and put a date on it. Then I schedule a time to do emotional processing with the assistance of a journal, a friend, a therapist or whatever kind of support works best for me. See pages 46-47.

Stays: If I have finished clearing the cluttered area, I can put back the things that truly belong in that space. I may want to set them up differently than I did before. If I run out of time, I put the box aside and schedule a time in the near future to complete the project.

I separate efficient sorting time from emotional processing time.

I build closure into every de-cluttering session.

I keep adjusting the plan so it fits me.

Specific Things to Try

Think of somebody from your past who was a really helpful boss, teacher, grandparent, or mentor of some kind. Describe all the positive things you remember about them. If you can't think of anyone like that from your own history, borrow from the movies, or a book, or your own imagination. What kind of person (or group of people) would be the perfect support for you as you face off with your clutter?

Make a list of five cluttered areas in your life. Limit their size. Focus on a drawer or surface – not the whole room.

1. _____

2. _____

3. _____

4. _____

5. _____

Choose one that bugs you every day but doesn't feel emotionally overwhelming. Imagine using the method described on pages 26-28 to address that area. Do you think it would work for you? Why or why not?

Notice if you feel like putting the experiment into action. If so, go ahead and try it, picturing your "helpful boss" or group of ideal support people cheering you on. Feel free to adjust the system so that it works for you. Once you've tried it, make some notes here about how it went.

Making Peace

The Anger Underneath the Clutter

All of my clutter is not angry clutter.
Some of it is just absent-minded.
Some is overwhelmed.
Some is hanging on for dear life.
Some is sorrowful.
But it is the angry clutter that says what I am not allowed to say.

I need space!
This is mine!
Keep out!
My territory!
Leave me alone!
You can't control me!
You can't tell me how to live!
Give me some attention!
Engage with me!
I want some respect!
I want you to listen!

Of course I would never say such things.
If I did the world would fall apart.
Crack in two.
No one would love me.
After all, I'm not supposed to have needs, wants, or desires.
I am not supposed to get angry.

So instead I take over each room in the house with
My Stuff.

I make messes I forget to clean up.
I mark my space with magazines and newspapers and
books I'm intending to read,
and fill spaces so full that there is no room
for anyone else's things.

And I go on being good,
and kind,
and reasonable,
and always, always pleasant.

A More Balanced Image of Order

Inside of me there is a character named Alexandria. She is the part of me that hates what she sees as tedious, unimportant tasks. She wants life to be exciting and dramatic. She wants every moment to have a golden glow. Housework, sorting and filling are like torture for her, and she sees no use in them at all. Yet she's totally in her glory when she's stirring things up, blazing a new trail, or when she has the attention of a crowd.

However, there is another part of me that loves those unglamorous tasks. She finds peace in sorting her cupboards and drawers. Crossing items off a to-do list gives her great satisfaction. She loves predictable routines, and a place for everything and everything in its place. I call this part of myself Gertrude.

Sometimes these two parts of my personality come to an impasse, or collide head on. I can tell this is happening when I procrastinate, spin my wheels, or feel blocked or stuck in some way. When I am about to take a risk, face an adventure or performance, Gertrude is likely to do her best to convince me that I really ought to be home getting my life in order instead of foolishly risking my life or embarrassing myself. Gertrude may be trying to help me balance my checkbook, but Alexandria is bored stiff, doing everything in her power to distract me and convince me that paperwork is a waste of time.

Alexandria and Gertrude represent two basic energies in the universe. Alexandria is chaos, freedom, spontaneity. Gertrude is order, structure, predictability. Each one feels that her way of being in the world is the right way.

Where there is no orderly energy whatsoever, there tends to be destructive chaos with structures being torn apart, or a limp, lethargic lack of direction. Too much order leads to rigidity, stagnation, and intolerance. Each extreme makes me long for the other. Confined by a rigid structure, I want freedom. Bombarded by chaos, I yearn for nothing but blessed order. Yet it is the balanced dance between chaos and order that allows life to flourish and enables creative dreams to manifest. It is what creates planets, holds them together, and keeps them in their orbits. It is what holds our bodies together and keeps them growing and changing.

Some of us have grown up with a particularly rigid Gertrude figure looming on our horizon. It may have been a mother or father, a fastidious uncle or plastic-slipcovers-on-all-the-furniture aunt, who was so concerned with order and neatness and the correct way of doing things that they drained every bit of fun out of life.

Why would we want to associate ourselves with that? Instead we decide to emphasize other sides of ourselves. The creative, fun-loving part of us plays the starring role in our lives. We focus on being easy-going and friendly, or wild and unpredictable. The orderly energy gets associated with all that is evil and life-killing, so we do our best to push it away.

Women have a particularly good reason to have spent their lives avoiding Gertrude energy. For generations we have been conditioned to believe that our bodies are only good for pleasing men, bearing children, and scrubbing floors. Many of us have been, or were raised by mothers who were going stir-crazy because their brilliant minds were being wasted on deciding which toilet bowl cleaner to use. We may equate caring for our homes, the orderly tasks of life, Gertrude energy, with the oppression of our dreams. In our minds, household chores stand in direct opposition to a successful professional life, a creative life, a life of satisfaction, passion and freedom. For many women, orderly energy means being a boring drudge with no life of her own.

But men may also carry negative images of order. They may have experienced a sadistic drill sergeant, an abusively anal boss, a boring, compulsive, humorless co-worker. Since housework has traditionally been considered a woman's job, many men grow up learning to avoid it and see it as demeaning and unworthy of their time and energy. Often it simply doesn't register as something to think about at all.

When we have these negative feelings attached to order, it's no wonder so many of us go in the other direction. That is unfortunate. Orderly energy is essential. When it is discounted, it turns nasty, becomes an annihilator, a critical inner voice that relentlessly nips every dream in the bud.

Chaos and order each need a place in my life, and they need to be in balance with each other. That is why I've been working for some time on creating welcoming space inside myself for both Alexandria and Gertrude. That has been an essential first step. Over time these two inner parts have even started listening to each other.

Alexandria is learning from Gertrude that putting her files and cupboards in order can be a way of putting her mind in order, and that putting some systems in place in her home can be a great support to her work and play out in the world. She is learning that life doesn't have to be so scattered and chaotic. Instead of dismissing them as unimportant, she is beginning to value the daily tasks that clothe, feed and shelter humanity.

Gertrude is learning from Alexandria that there is more to life than just keeping her house in order. There comes a time to venture out into the world. If she hides out too long making lists and wiping counters, she is likely to become obsessed with dust and mildew and forget the bigger picture. This planet needs all the help it can get, and it may require that her little light shine in a bigger arena than her own four walls.

Somewhere between Alexandria and Gertrude is a more balanced image of order. Lately I've been experimenting with bringing these two together.

I put on music and sing loudly while sweeping the floor.

I work on a creative project, get stuck, and then shift to folding laundry and putting it away. By the time I'm finished my creative juices are flowing again.

I take the time to prepare carefully for a presentation. I allow for all the little details instead of rushing out the door late with my hair still wet.

I have some open time and I feel daunted by a long "To Do" list. Instead of avoiding it, I throw ten "To Do" items into a hat, along with a few fun activities. Then I draw one, allowing the fates to help me decide what to focus on first, and to playfully guide me through my day.

All of these are signs that Alexandria and Gertrude are working together on my behalf.

The more I honor each of their energies, valuing what gifts they bring, the more they seem to be willing to cooperate with each other and with me. That opens up a world of possibilities.

Housecleaning

It is an energetic act,
an intentional act,
polishing,
dusting,
rubbing surfaces,
shaking things out,
changing everything from dull gray to bright white,
from muffled brown to rich mahogany,
savoring the sensual difference between stiff, stinky socks,
and soft warm laundry in smooth folds.

I put on music and do every movement rhythmically,
choose my cleaning music as if for dancing.

Sometimes though, it is the quiet I like,
the quiet of a house after everyone has left,
blessing each corner and making it new,
letting the light in.

I am not a whipped workhorse, plodding in circles.
I am an alchemist, transforming my life as I transform this space.

It could be compulsive, but it needn't be.
Reorganizing the cupboards,
I do some rearranging of my life.
Getting rid of the dead cereal boxes,
I get rid of some of my own dead weight.
Cleaning up the spilled soap under the sink
my mind feels more clear.

We cannot be forever creative,
witty, intelligent,
dazzling, and interesting.

Sometimes the routine,
the gentle tending of our homes
is just the thing for a weary soul.

Specific Things to Try

When you decide to Confront your Clutter, there is likely to be inner conflict. There may be a part of you that wants to sabotage the process. It isn't necessarily ill-intentioned. It may sincerely believe that your clutter is doing good things for you. Imagine that part. How might it try to convince you to hang onto the things you are considering releasing? What arguments might it use to justify its position? After reading over these examples, add some of your own.

You never know. I might need it.

It helps me to remember things I've done and places I've been.

It reminds me of the people I love and have lost.

_____

_____

_____

_____

_____

_____

Look over the examples I gave and the arguments you added. Circle three of them that feel especially relevant for you. If you think of these as related to legitimate needs, what would those needs be? Examples might include *safety, a sense of identity,* or *connection to others.* Try completing the sentence below in three different ways.

My clutter is trying to address my need for _____

My clutter is trying to address my need for _____

My clutter is trying to address my need for _____

What if you took those needs seriously? Are there better ways of addressing them? For example, someone concerned about safety and being prepared could intentionally put together an emergency kit that would directly address their fears. That might eliminate the need to try to save everything "just in case." List below some things you could do to more effectively honor the needs your clutter is trying to meet.

1. _____

2. _____

3. _____

Now imagine that there is a part of you that is totally convinced it's time to get rid of the clutter. What are some of the arguments that part would make? Here are some examples. Add some of your own.

It depresses me and drains my energy.

It's embarrassing.

_____

_____

_____

_____

_____

_____

You might want to imagine these two parts of yourself meeting somewhere neutral to have a peaceful and constructive discussion. Begin to open to the possibility that they could actually respect each other's viewpoints and work together to meet your needs. You may even want to create a dialogue between the two of them. You can write it out as if it were a movie script.

Releasing

Letting Go

The need to let go always takes me by surprise, even though it happens over and over again in my life. I just came through yet another letting go experience. I was sick. I wasn't deathly ill. I just had a bad cold that lasted about a week, but it carried with it all the stages of grief.

First I went through denial. "I can't be getting sick," I said to myself as I coughed and trembled. "I don't have time to be sick." So my body spoke more loudly, causing me to wilt with fatigue. "Okay," I admitted. "Maybe I have a one-day bug." I bargained next. "I'll go to bed now, but I'd better be well in time for my rehearsal." Of course I wasn't, and I realized I was going to have to call all of my clients and cancel for the following day as well.

It is sad to have to let go. After all, life is for living. I want to act, do, engage, and be productive. It seems like defeat to go back to bed. Occasionally though, I have to remember that the world can go on without me. I also have to remember that letting go is a natural part of living. I re-learn these things painfully every time I get sick.

Once I remember these things, it is okay. Sometimes I even take some pleasure in letting go. I rest and recharge my batteries. I slow down and listen to my body. I read the books I have been meaning to get to. I sleep and sleep. I often feel that at such times I am checking out of the world so that something can heal on a deeper level. When I allow my body its natural healing process, I always come out of it with a renewed appreciation and enthusiasm for simply being alive.

Confronting Clutter requires a lot of letting go. Many of us resist that. We so easily get into the mode of accumulating, saving, preparing, getting good deals. We rescue things that might have been thrown away by others. These activities can feel lively and exhilarating.

Then, one day we notice that the closet door won't close and things are spilling out of the cupboards. The basement is filling up. It no longer feels pleasant to walk into the house, or comfortable to have friends over. It is time to let go.

For many of us, this comes as a shock. It goes against all our programming to start getting rid of the things we've so actively accumulated. Shifting gears into letting go mode can be jarring and uncomfortable.

Eventually, we may remember that it is also a very important part of life. Like weeding the garden, pruning the deadwood, letting go allows new life to grow.

My Journals

I have been keeping journals for twenty-four years -
ninety-three of them, spiral-bound
sketch pads with no lines.

I open one up and there is my twenty-one-year-old self
naming her truth, finding her voice.
I open another and my thirty-nine-year-old self is writing poetry
about chaos and order.

I want to preserve them –
To line them up chronologically in a wooden cabinet with
glass doors and a golden key.

 I turn the page and remember now
that these are unedited journals –
that filling the space between strokes of brilliance are pages of
dull drivel, fatigue, envy,
a thousand recipes for self-improvement,
and infinite incriminating items I would hate
for my loved ones to discover.

Putrid, unsightly, this is the fertilizer for my life,
my relationships, my creations.
I want to put my journals in the compost pile,
bury them deep,
and invite the worms to have their fill.

These spiral sketchbooks hold all of me –
the writer who wants to mine them for gems,
the lazy one who can't be bothered,
the old woman who wants to look back,
the embarrassed one who wants to forget.

Right now they sit in cardboard boxes in an old wooden garage
surrounded by things we don't know how to keep and
don't know how to let go.

I worry that they are decomposing,
even as I wait, impatiently, for them to turn back into soil.

Specific Things to Try

Focus on an object that would be a likely candidate for the Emotional Box (described on pages 26 and 28). It may be something that represents a chapter of your life that ended badly. It may be connected to some activity you used to do, or a gift you are keeping out of guilt, or one of the many things left behind by a loved one who has died. It may be one object that represents a whole category of your belongings. Make sure it is something that you don't know whether to keep or let go. Write about the object, how it came into your life, and what it represents for you.

What feelings do you experience when you look at the object now?

Try springing off of the phrase, "*If I keep it . . .*" Let your imagination run wild. Don't worry if one sentence conflicts with the next. Get all the feelings down. If you don't feel like writing, try drawing something that visually expresses your hopes and fears about keeping it. Write fast so your inner critic can't get in the way.

> *If I keep it I would like to put it in a beautiful display cabinet and pass it down to my loved ones who would pass it down to their loved ones for generations. If I keep it, I will feel burdened and stuck. If I keep it I don't know where to put it. If I keep it everyone will admire it and think I'm an ∧interesting, unique person. . .*
>
> *If I keep it . . .*

Now try springing off of the phrase, "*If I let it go . . .*" Make room for all the hopes and fears and contradictions that are inside you.

If I let it go I'll regret it forever. They'll never forgive me. It will be the thing I absolutely need the most and I won't have it. I'll forget about it. I won't care. I'll move on with my life feeling lighter and freer. If I let it go . . .

If I let it go . . .

Notice if you have any more clarity about what to do after doing these writings. Fortunately, it isn't necessary to write about every piece of clutter. Taking the time to deeply explore a few sample objects can clear some mental and emotional clutter, and often help you know what action to take with that item, and with others that are in a similar category.

If You've Had a Recent Loss don't expect yourself to jump too quickly into deciding what to keep and what to let go. If you've lost someone very close to you it may help to box up the person's things and go through them, with support, when some time has passed. Or you can create an art piece or shrine of remembrance, incorporating some particularly meaningful objects. When the time is right you can share some of the things with others who would find them meaningful, and donate to charities your loved one would wish to support. Enlist the help of friends, relatives, or professionals who are supportive, respectful, and have good ideas. Whether you've lost a person, a job, a home or something else very dear to you, do your best to treat yourself with patience and kindness, letting go in your own time and way.

Navigating
Time

Time Clutter

It is just as easy for me to clutter my schedule
as it is for me to clutter my space.
Just like with money, space, energy, information,
I can tend to think that
More
will solve everything.

If I only had more time
then there wouldn't be a problem.
I would put everything away when I was finished.
I'd make careful choices when I shopped
so I wouldn't end up with so much junk.
All those things around the house that don't work
I'd take the time to repair or return,
and I could always find the warranty.
There would be no more dishes in the sink,
no more papers on my desk,
and all of my photos would be carefully arranged in albums,
in chronological order,
with humorous captions.

I tell myself that someday I will have time.
On the weekend.
Next month, when things slow down.
When my vacation comes around.
When I'm financially independent.
Then, I'll get right to it.

But right now my calendar is packed.
There's not a bit of space in it.
And all of it is important
so I can't possibly deal with anything as trivial as
clutter.

And when I say these things to myself,
I actually believe they are true.

Three Versions of Time Hell

Time Hell Number One

I am driving to the grocery store hoping it will take zero time. In fact, I'm counting on it taking zero time. I operate on the premise that if I were really efficient, if I made every stop light, and nobody else was waiting in the check-out line, then I could get to the store and back without any time passing. I look at my watch cursing every movement of the second hand. I groan at every red light. I am furious at all the people waiting in the check-out line.

When I walk in my front door I look miserably at the clock which makes no bones about the fact that I will be late getting to my next appointment. I rush out the door, the clock chasing me and breathing down my neck, and once again I am desperately hoping that this drive will take zero time.

This is one way I can imprison myself with time. I cram in more activities than are humanly possible. I treat myself like a machine, or the victim of the all-powerful clock, my oppressive slave-driver. I spend an entire day acting as if time is after me. I buzz around from activity to activity, never truly sinking in or connecting to anything. A visit with a friend becomes an item to be checked off a list. I can pant instead of breathe. I come to the end of the day with a rattled mind and an empty heart.

Time Hell Number Two

I am pretending time doesn't exist. Work starts a little later for me today, but I am acting like I have endless hours. I stay in bed a long time. I have a big breakfast. Instead of making the three quick phone calls that been hanging over me, I have a long, shooting-the-breeze conversation with a friend. I pick up a magazine and dreamily get lost in an article.

Suddenly it's time to go to work and of course I have not done any of the preparations. A minute ago time didn't exist at all. Now it's crashing down on me like a sledge hammer. I race around wildly, ripping clothes off of hangers, tripping over my shoes. After five minutes of turning my home into a disaster area and a harrowing drive at break-neck speed, I arrive late to work with nothing to eat, no checks in my checkbook, wearing an outfit I don't like at all, and feeling completely unready to face this day.

This method of abusing myself with time does have its benefits. For awhile I get to disconnect from time and do whatever I want. But this quick jerking into another mode is deeply taxing to my body and my mind, and also does a real number on my self-esteem. I spend the remainder of the day stressed, having lost all the helpful benefits of my relaxing morning.

Time Hell Number Three

Time stretches before me. An entire day, all to myself, with no commitments to anybody else. Time to catch up on all the little things I've been putting off. A luxurious day I've been looking forward to for so long. I have that delicious feeling I used to get when my mother would decide I was just sick enough to stay home from school. Yet it's also a day bursting with potential.

Something about all that potential becomes unnerving as the day wears on. I get caught between feeling like it's okay to rest, and the pressure to be accomplishing things. I find myself filling up the time in ways I hadn't meant to, gazing into the fridge, flipping on the TV, shopping for things I don't really need. The afternoon begins to taste like a stale cracker and the coming of dusk leaves me with a feeling of melancholy. I had wanted wondrous things to spring from this day. Now that time is mine, all I seem to be able to do is waste it.

This is a particularly distressing version of Time Hell because it shatters my illusion that "if I only had enough time," everything would be perfect. I am faced with the fact that I don't really have a clear idea how to use this gift of time. Because I never made a real choice about the focus of this day I come to the end of it without feeling rested, without the glow of accomplishment and productivity, having had no fun, no spark of adventure or risk, and without the joy of creativity and self-expression.

Befriending Time

For too much of my life, time has been my enemy. When I have wanted to move slowly, it has chased me. When I've wanted to ignore it, it has sprung up in my face like a jack-in-the-box. When I've wanted the moments to zip along, time has dragged relentlessly.

Time is my enemy when I show up with a mindset that does not fit the occasion, as if overdressed or underdressed for a party. It does me no good to take a vacation if I'm still stuck in the checking-items-off-a-list mentality that was so helpful when I was preparing to get away. If I'm in savoring-the-moment mode, that relaxed dreaminess can be of no use at all in getting through a tedious stack of paperwork or a long list of phone calls.

Time is also my enemy when I never stop and clearly decide what it is I am doing with it; giving this day or this hour or this moment a title. When I get pulled towards rest and pulled towards responsibility, ending up stretched and depleted with nothing to show for it, I often blame time. That is unfair. Time is what it is. I can choose to be its victim or to befriend it and work with it creatively.

Many things are endless. Housework is endless. The needs of other people are endless. But my time, energy and tolerance are not endless. I have to set limits somewhere, so I might as well set them in a way that leaves me feeling more sane, and more able to complete tasks, instead of harried, with a lot of loose ends dangling. To do so makes time seem a little friendlier.

Another way I can befriend time is to introduce little extra spaces into my schedule. I build in breathing space to bring closure to one project before starting another, or for the inevitable monkey wrench that tends to fly into the midst of my careful plans.

I am also trying to build in some longer spaces of time when I don't have to be productive or accountable to anyone else. In a world full of digital watches, computers, cell phones, traffic and deadlines, it is crucial to my health that I regularly take time to shift into following the rhythms of my own body. I need to remember that I am a creature and not a machine. I breathe. My blood flows. I have emotions and dreams, sweat and songs, and they need to move through me.

To make this shift into relaxing rejuvenating time I require some extra help; a transition ritual. It can be as simple as a bath, dancing, gathering with friends, breathing into my belly, or going out into a cold night and opening my eyes and my heart to a sky full of stars.

Befriending time also means learning to do one thing at a time, fully, and with presence. This is easiest for me when I am moving slowly, carefully examining each leaf and twig of my inner and outer landscapes. These days I have that luxury, but I don't count on that lasting. I live in a culture that moves rapidly, and in a universe that mixes chaos with order to keep things lively and interesting. I understand that the shape of my life can change any moment, the pace increasing and the pressure intensifying.

In karate class, we always practice each series of movements twice, first *slowly, for form*, where we pay attention to every little subtlety. We notice the posture, the bend of the knee, and angle of the wrist. Then we do it *up to speed*, and I have to challenge my muscles to move faster than I believe they can move. My mind tends to panic and wail, "This is impossible!" Often my chin is jutting out, I'm rising up high instead of staying low and grounded, and I'm losing my balance at every turn. There are no more distinct movements. It has all become an ambiguous blur. Yet the challenge is to continue to do one thing at a time, and to increase the focus.

Right now I am living my life *slowly, for form*. I am trying to pay attention to the subtleties. I am learning to do one thing at a time and working on bringing integrity to each moment. Even in slow motion I sometimes stumble, like a centipede trying to keep track of her feet. All around me people are living their lives *up to speed*. They whiz past me, some quite sloppy, flopping all over the place, some appearing to be extremely efficient, graceful, and fully focused. It can be intimidating. It can throw off my rhythm. Still I keep practicing my moves.

When the pace increases, chaos enters the scene, and my life is suddenly upended, I am certain that I will sometimes tilt, wobble, lose my balance, and even lose myself in the panic to get everything done. But I am encouraged. I am learning that practicing *slowly, for form* pays off. My karate is improving, and now even when we are moving *up to speed* I can feel myself being a little stronger, more graceful, bringing more definition to each movement.

Slowly, over time, it is beginning to feel more natural to increase the focus when the pressure increases, to quiet the mind when the panic starts to rise, and to breathe in spaciousness when my anxiety tells me to be tight and rigid. As that shift begins to take place, time feels less and less like an enemy, and more and more like a friend.

Specific Things to Try

Describe a version of "Time Hell" that you experience fairly often.

What would you need to shift in order to have the above situation go better?

Imagine that you have all the time in the world with no immediate obligations hounding you. How do you imagine yourself spending that precious time? Think about what would bring you the most joy and would have the most meaning for you. Don't worry about answering this in the perfect way. Just notice what you think and feel today. Set a timer and write for five minutes or write until you've filled this space. Don't edit or think too hard. Let it come out however it wants to.

What are the obstacles keeping you from spending time the way you just described? What kinds of physical, mental, and emotional clutter are in the way? What habits or commitments are using up the time that could be devoted to more satisfying pursuits? Again, set a timer and write for five minutes or write until you've filled this space.

Are there any changes that you feel willing to make in order to improve your relationship with time? If so, what are they?

How can you be a kind, encouraging "helpful boss" to yourself while teaching yourself to do things differently?

Confronting
Clutter
Concepts

Clutter costs time, money, space and energy.

Clutter is expensive. It wastes my time when I'm frantically looking for lost items or trying to clean around my piles. It wastes my money when I have to move it, store it, or purchase a duplicate of some item I can't find in the clutter. It exhausts me physically to navigate around it, pushing things out of the way every time I want to start a project. It drains me psychologically, reinforcing negative feelings about myself. This is important to remember when I am caught up in telling myself all my reasons for keeping something.

Each person needs to let go of clutter at their own pace.

I have learned never to assume I fully understand why another person has clutter. For some it is a light, funny annoyance. For some it is a heavy, lifelong issue attached to intense trauma and loss. For some it's linked to a challenging life transition. People dealing with clutter need encouragement and support, not intrusiveness and harsh judgment. It is best if each of us can do it in our own way and time. Sometimes in emergency situations this is not possible, but we and our belongings still need to be treated with as much respect as possible.

Once we get past the point of "enough," more stuff makes life more difficult.

Every day we hear the message that more stuff will make our lives better. The reality is that more stuff often means more to trip over, more to lose, and more to feel guilty about neglecting.

Clutter keeps us emotionally bound to the past and the future. To confront our clutter frees up energy for living more fully in the present.

I don't have to get rid of everything I'm saving from my past. It's fine for me to accumulate some things for the future. However, if most of my living space is occupied with artifacts from every chapter of my life and piles of things I might need someday, it's time to start weeding out and making space for the here and now.

We are constantly evolving, moving from one stage of life to another. When we release the things that don't fit us anymore we can open the way for unexpected blessings.

If I am willing to stop gripping my belongings in fear, my hands can be open to receive the gifts that are coming my way.

A Closing Message

If you have read through this book, good for you. Maybe you haven't let go of one thing while reading it. Still, it counts as progress that you've taken some time to consciously focus on this part of your life. You may find that you're starting to think about your clutter in different ways. You may even feel a little less shame and a little more inspiration.

If you've gotten yourself to do some of the exercises, that's even better. The kind of process writing you've been doing engages many parts of the brain and helps bring clarity where there has been confusion. By working in this way you have made a start in clearing some of the mental and emotional clutter that contributes to the physical and time clutter.

You may have started taking action. Maybe you have cleared some spaces, let go of some excess baggage, or made some helpful changes in your schedule. That's wonderful. You are well on your way and may be getting to take pleasure in some of the changes.

No matter where you are in the process of Confronting Your Clutter, take a moment now to think about your next step. What will help you keep this momentum going? Is there someone you can check in with regularly to keep you motivated? Is there a class or support group you can join? Is there a friend you can trade time with? Are there items on the resource list that it would be good to check out? Maybe you feel ready for a more detailed, step-by-step organizing book. It may be time to go back to some of the exercises in this book and do the ones you skipped before. Whatever your next step, it helps to picture yourself following through with it.

You get to Confront the Clutter in your life in your own time and way, supported by people, tools and resources that are genuinely helpful to you. It is not about fitting someone else's mold of who you are supposed to be. It's about claiming your life. You deserve to do that, and the good news is that you don't have to do it perfectly.

Forgive yourself for the current state of things. Inspire yourself with a compelling vision. Give yourself the kinds of support that tend to help you make change. Above all, remember that this is a process and do your best to be kind and encouraging to yourself every step of the way. That is the best recipe I know for successfully Confronting Your Clutter.

Resources

Books

Adams, Kathleen. *Journal to the Self.* New York, N.Y.: Hachette Book Group, 1990.

Debroitner, Rita Kirsch and Avery Hart. *Moving Beyond ADD/ADHD.* Kill Devil Hills, NC: Transpersonal Publishing, 2007.

Glovinsky, Cindy. *Making Peace with the Things in Your Life.* New York, N.Y.: St. Martin's Press, 2002.

_____,*One Thing at a Time; 100 Simple Ways to Live Clutter-Free Every Day.* New York, N.Y.: St. Martin's Press, 2004.

Kingston, Karen. *Clear Your Clutter with Feng Shui.* New York, N.Y.: Random House, 1999.

Kolberg, Judith. *Conquering Chronic Disorganization* (second edition). Decatur, GA: Squall Press, 2007.

and Kathleen Nadeau. *ADD-Friendly Ways to Organize Your Life.* New York, N.Y.: Brunner-Routledge, 2002.

Marcus, Clare Cooper. *House as a Mirror of Self.* Berkeley, CA: Conari Press, 1995.

Morgenstern, Julie. *Organizing from the Inside Out.* New York, N.Y.: Henry Holt and Company, Inc., 1998.

_____,*Time Management from the Inside Out.* New York, N.Y.: Henry Holt and Company, 2000.

_____, *When Organizing Isn't Enough – SHED Your Stuff, Change Your Life.* New York, NY: Simon & Schuster, Inc., 2008

Tolin, David, Randy Frost and Gail Steketee. *Buried in Treasures: Help for Compulsive Acquiring, Saving and Hoarding.* New York, N.Y.: Oxford University Press, 2007.

Websites

Carolyn Koehnline: www.ConfrontingClutter.com

Craig's List: An easy way to sell things on-line. http://www.craigslist.com

Emotional Freedom Technique (EFT): A method to quickly decrease anxiety and self-sabotaging behaviors. http://www.emofree.com

Fly Lady: She breaks household maintenance down into little steps and gives humorous reminders each day about what to focus on. http://www.flylady.net

Freecycle: A great place to let people know you have something to give away free. http://www.freecycle.org

Clutterers Anonymous: http://www.clutterers-anonymous.org

Messies Anonymous: http://www.messies.com/

National Association of Professional Organizers: http://www.napo.net/

National Attention Deficit Disorder Association: http://www.add.org/

ADDvance: An on-line magazine for women with ADD. http://www.addvance.com

OCD Resource Center: http://www.ocdresources.com

CPSIA information can be obtained
at www.ICGtesting.com
Printed in the USA
LVOW09s0130160517
534666LV00031B/885/P